The Little Black Book of Classroom Management

Essential Wisdom for Educators

Frances Watson Hester, Ph.D.

Copyright Notice

Copyright © 2025 Frances Watson Hester, Ph.D.

All rights reserved. No part of this publication may be copied, reproduced, republished, translated, stored, or transmitted in any form or by any means whether electronic, mechanical, digital, or otherwise - without the prior written permission of the publisher.

This book is the result of dedication, creativity, and countless hours of effort. Any resemblance to real persons, living or dead, is purely coincidental or perhaps just the universe having a bit of fun.

Published by Kinetic Digital Publishers

www.kineticdigitalpublishers.com

For permissions, inquiries, or other correspondence, please visit our website.

ISBN:
eBook: 978-0-9993773-4-5
Paperback: 978-0-9993773-3-8
Hardcover: 978-0-9993773-5-2

Foreword

By Robert Jackson, National Speaker and Author

I've worked with educators across the U.S. and Canada for over 20 years. In that time, I've met countless professionals who talk a good game about transforming education. But rarely do I meet someone who walks the walk with the authenticity, grit, and unwavering commitment that Dr. Frances Watson-Hester brings to every classroom, every school, and every student she touches.

When Dr. Hester speaks, educators listen—not because of her impressive titles or accolades (though she has plenty), but because she embodies a truth too many have forgotten: it's not about systems, policies, or even curriculum. It's about the relationships we build and the environments we create.

I first encountered Dr. Hester's work through her earlier publications. I was immediately struck by her fearless approach to addressing what she calls "the elephant in the room." While others tiptoe around tough conversations—about student behavior, classroom management, and educational equity—Frances charges straight in with real solutions. Solutions that don't just sound good on paper—they work in practice, because she's tested them in the trenches.

The Little Black Book of Classroom Management isn't another abstract framework detached from classroom realities. It's a practitioner's guide written by someone who's been there—who has faced the Monday mornings that make educators question their calling, who has seen the spark of potential in students' others have labeled "difficult," and who has built bridges between what we know works and what actually happens in schools.

What sets this book apart is Dr. Hester's unwavering belief

that every child can succeed—when we, the adults, get our act together. She doesn't entertain excuses or deflection. Instead, she offers concrete strategies, honest reflection, and practical tools that can transform not just classrooms, but careers.

Throughout these pages, you'll discover that classroom management isn't about control—it's about connection. You'll learn that your most challenging students often become your greatest success stories when you approach them with intentionality instead of frustration. And you'll be reminded of why you entered this field in the first place: to change lives.

Dr. Hester's voice resonates because it comes from a place of deep love for students and profound respect for educators. She understands that teaching is one of the most demanding—and most important—professions on earth. She honors that challenge by offering tools that actually work in the real world of public education. She has worked in leadership as a teacher, counselor, assistant principal and principal. I have seen her character and work ethic up close and personal because I have worked with her schools when she served as principal.

As you read this book, prepare to be challenged, inspired, and equipped. Dr. Hester won't let you settle for mediocrity or accept systems that fail our kids. Instead, she'll show you how to become the educator every child deserves—the one who sees potential where others see problems, who builds bridges where others see barriers.

The future of education won't be written in policy papers or boardrooms. It's being written right now—in the daily choices of educators who show up, build relationships, and never give up on any child. With this book in your hands, you're already on the right path.

Our students are counting on us to get this right. And with Dr. Hester as your guide, you will.

Robert Jackson is a renowned educational consultant and best-selling author. He has inspired educators across the nation and abroad to reclaim their power to transform lives through intentional teaching practices.

Dedication

To my beloved Aunt Dorothy Jean Watson (T Dorothy)

(October 28, 1952 – September 20, 2024)

This book is lovingly dedicated to the memory of Dorothy Jean Watson, whose extraordinary life illuminated the path for countless educators and students. From her early brilliance as Salutatorian of Martin High School's Class of 1969 at just sixteen years old, to her groundbreaking tenure as the first Black woman to serve as School Board President in Catahoula Parish, T Dorothy embodied the transformative power of education and unwavering dedication to justice.

For forty seven remarkable years, she graced the Franklin Parish School System with her presence, ascending from secretary to district Supervisor—each role a testament to her belief that every child deserves excellence in education. Her three degrees from Grambling State University reflected not just personal achievement, but a commitment to lifelong learning that she instilled in everyone she encountered.

T Dorothy, you were truly "the light of the world" that Matthew 5:14-16 speaks of—a beacon whose light could never be hidden. Your good deeds continue to glorify our heavenly Father through the lives you touched, the minds you shaped, and the barriers you broke. Your legacy of advocacy for change, equality, and justice lives on in every classroom where a teacher refuses to give up on a child, in every school board meeting where courage speaks truth, and in every educational leader who remembers that our calling is sacred.

This work on classroom management is inspired by your example—that true education is not just about managing a classroom, but about nurturing souls, championing equity, and lighting the way for future generations. May your spirit of excellence, your heart for service, and your unwavering faith continue to guide educators everywhere.

Your light continues to shine, dear T Dorothy. Thank you for showing us the way.

With deepest love and eternal gratitude,

Frances Watson-Hester, Ph.D.

TABLE OF CONTENTS

Foreword i
By Robert Jackson, National Speaker and Author
Dedication iv
Introduction 1
First Impressions Matter 3
Establishing Authority 6
Building Community as a Nonnegotiable 8
Physical Environment 12
Essential Routines 15
Attention Signals 18
Transitions That Work 20
Managing Materials 22
Group Work Strategies 24
Digital Classroom Management 26
Voice and Body Language 28
The Power of Proximity 30
Addressing Minor Disruptions 32
De-escalation Techniques 34
Promoting Student Accountability 36
Building Student Relationships 38
Managing Different Personalities 40
Clear Communication 43

Time Management Mastery 45
Parent Partnerships 47
Cultural Responsiveness 49
Trauma-Informed Approaches 51
Self-Care and Sustainability 53
Emergency Responses 55
Final Thoughts 57

Introduction

This Little Black Book contains hard-earned wisdom from decades in the classroom. These are not theoretical ideals, but battle-tested strategies that work in real classrooms with real students. Keep this guide close—it may save your sanity on the toughest days.

Remember: Effective classroom management is never about controlling students. It's about creating conditions where learning thrives and students develop self-regulation. Every strategy in this book serves that ultimate purpose.

"Every student who walks through your door carries the potential to change the world. Your first impression of them—and theirs of you—may determine whether that potential flourish or remains dormant."

Frances Watson-Hester, Ph.D.

Teacher Affirmation

"I am a curator of possibilities. Each day, I choose to see the spark in every student, even when it's hidden beneath layers of doubt or defiance. My classroom is where dreams take their first brave steps toward reality."

Frances Watson Hester, Ph.D.

First Impressions Matter

Day One Essentials

- Be at the door: Greet each student personally as they enter.

- Start with structure: Have an activity ready for students the moment they arrive.

- Introduce yourself strategically: Share enough to be human but maintain professional boundaries.

- Establish three non-negotiable expectations: Too many rules create confusion; focus on what matters most.

- Create a treatment agreement with your class community. This will define the way they will treat/respect each other daily. Post it on the wall and review it daily as part of your daily routine. This agreement can change if needed. Once all students agree to 3-5 items, the teacher and all students will sign the treatment agreement. This creates a safe place for learning and treating each other with respect.

- Practice procedures immediately: Don't just explain—rehearse.

- Introduce your students to daily check in'-ins, check up'-ups, and check out'-outs times to ensure that they are learning and mentally ready throughout the day. Make this a part of your class culture. This builds empathy and compassion amongst the class community.

First Week Priorities

- Spend 30% of your time on content, 70% on procedures and relationships.
- Learn names within 48 hours—use name tents, seating charts, and mnemonic devices.
- Make positive phone calls home for at least two students per day.
- Observe student social dynamics closely during unstructured time.
- Pay attention to your student's body language.
- Build in weekly team builder activities with students to build peer to Implement weekly team-building activities with students to foster peer-to-peer relationships.
- End each day with a quick success to build momentum.

Common First Week Mistakes

Smiling too little (appears stern) or too much (appears insecure).

- Over-explaining procedures rather than practicing them.
- Rushing into the curriculum before foundations are solid.
- Reacting emotionally to testing behaviors.
- Failing to follow through on stated consequences.

"True authority whispers while insecurity shouts. The teacher who must demand respect has already lost it, but the one who earns it never needs to ask for it."

Frances Watson-Hester, Ph.D.

Teacher Affirmation

"My authority flows from competence, consistency, and care—not from control. I lead with confidence because I know my purpose: to guide, to inspire, and to believe in my students even when they don't believe in themselves."

Establishing Authority

Three Pillars of Authority

1. Expertise: Demonstrate deep knowledge of your subject.
2. Consistency: Apply expectations uniformly and reliably.
3. Authentic Care: Show genuine interest in student success.

Authority Destroyers

- Making threats you can't or won't enforce
- Engaging in power struggles publicly
- Showing favoritism (even unintentionally)
- Apologizing for enforcing reasonable expectations
- Allowing exceptions without a clear rationale

Rebuilding Authority When Challenged

- Address issues privately whenever possible.
- Use "press pause" language: "We'll discuss this after class."
- Separate the behavior from the student's worth.
- Provide a fresh start after addressing issues.
- Document patterns for future reference.

A classroom is not a collection of individual students—it is a community waiting to be born. The teacher who builds walls creates learners; the teacher who builds bridges creates leaders."

Frances Watson-Hester, Ph.D.

Teacher Affirmation

"I am a community architect, designing spaces where every voice matters and every heart belongs. When my students look around our classroom, they see not strangers, but family—each person valued, each contribution cherished."

Building Community as a Nonnegotiable

The Foundation of Community

- Community before curriculum: Academic success follows emotional safety and belonging.
- Deliberate design: Community doesn't happen by accident—it requires intentional structures.
- Ongoing process: Community building isn't a first-week activity, but a daily practice.
- Shared ownership: Students must contribute to the community vision and maintenance.
- Authentic connection: Real relationships cannot be replaced by management techniques.

Essential Community Structures

- Morning meetings/Advisory periods: Dedicated time for connection and community building
- Class agreements: Collaboratively created expectations for how we treat each other
- Conflict resolution protocols: Established processes for addressing interpersonal issues
- Recognition systems: Ways to acknowledge contributions to the community
- Celebration rituals: Regular acknowledgment of collective and individual achievements
- Feedback loops: Mechanisms for students to shape classroom culture

High-Impact Community Practices

- Identity sharing: Structured activities for students to share their backgrounds, interests, and strengths
- Collaborative problem-solving: Engaging students in addressing classroom challenges
- Cross-group connections: Intentionally mixing students beyond self-selected groups
- Class challenges: Collective goals that require everyone's contribution
- Service projects: Opportunities to contribute to the broader community
- Restorative circles: Addressing harm and rebuilding relationships when community norms are broken

Community Check-Up Questions

- Regularly assess your classroom community with these questions:
- Do all students have at least one meaningful connection with a peer?
- Can students articulate the purpose and value of class expectations?
- How do students respond when a classmate struggles or makes a mistake?
- Do students take initiative to solve problems or always rely on teacher intervention?
- Is participation distributed equitably across the classroom?
- Do students demonstrate care for the physical space and materials?

When Community Breaks Down

- Address divisions or exclusions immediately—they rarely resolve without intervention.
- Use neutral language to name community challenges: "I've noticed that..."
- Engage students in diagnosing and solving community problems.
- Rebuild after difficult incidents through structured activities that restore trust.
- Model vulnerability and repair when you've contributed to community breakdown.

"Your classroom's physical space speaks before you do. Every wall, every desk arrangement, every corner tells students whether they matter, whether learning is valued, and whether they belong."

Frances Watson-Hester, Ph.D.

Teacher Affirmation

"My classroom environment is my silent teaching partner. Every detail I choose—from where desks face to what adorns the walls—whispers to my students: 'You are expected, you are welcome, and great things happen here.'"

Physical Environment

Strategic Seating Arrangements

- Traditional rows: Maximizes teacher control, minimizes student interaction
- Pairs: Balances collaboration and individual focus
- Groups of four: Enhances discussion, but increases management challenges
- U-shape: Facilitates whole-class discussion and teacher movement
- Flexible: Varies based on activity (requires practiced transition systems)

Movement Mapping

- Create a classroom map and track your movement patterns for one day.
- Identify "dead zones" where you rarely visit.
- Design pathways that allow you to reach any student within 5 seconds.
- Place high-need students in locations with natural proximity.
- Create buffer zones around students who trigger each other.

Visual Environment Tips

- Minimize visual clutter, especially around instructional areas.
- Use consistent color-coding for subject areas or types of information.

- Post essential information at eye level; decorative elements higher.
- Include student work that demonstrates process, not just perfect products.
- Create dedicated spaces for daily information (objectives, homework, schedule).

"Excellence is not an act, but a habit. In education, routines are the daily deposits we make into the bank account of student success."

Frances Watson-Hester, Ph.D.

Teacher Affirmation

"I am a conductor of daily rhythms that create harmony from chaos. My routines are not restrictions—they are liberating structures that free my students' minds to focus on what matters most: learning, growing, and becoming."

Essential Routines

Beginning of Class

- Entry routine with immediate activity (bellwork, do-now, warm-up)
- Materials readiness check
- Objective and agenda review
- Connection to previous learning
- Clear start signal
- Ensure all students have materials to use daily. Don't depend on parents necessarily.

Ending Class

- Closure activity that synthesizes learning
- Exit ticket or formative assessment
- Materials organization and return
- Preview of next session
- Dismissal procedure (teacher dismisses, not the bell)

Materials Distribution

- Pre-positioned materials on desks
- Student materials managers
- Table captains or row leaders
- Numbered or color-coded systems
- Digital distribution for paperless options

Managing Incomplete Work

- Designated a physical or digital space for missing assignments
- Documentation system that students can access independently
- Regular opportunity for completion during designated times
- Clear communication system for sharing with families
- Recognition for responsibility (not just completion)

"In the symphony of learning, the teacher's attention signal is not the conductor's baton demanding silence—it is the gentle tuning fork that brings all instruments into harmony."

Frances Watson-Hester, Ph.D.

Teacher Affirmation

"My voice carries the power to unite twenty-five different worlds into one shared moment of learning. When I call for attention, I'm not demanding compliance—I'm inviting connection to something beautiful we're creating together."

Attention Signals

Multi-Sensory Signals

1. Visual: Raised hand, light flickering, timer display
2. Auditory: Chimes, clapping pattern, verbal cue
3. Kinesthetic: Physical gesture that students mirror

Training for Response

- Explain the signal and expected response
- Practice when attention is already focused
- Practice during minor distractions
- Practice during active engagement
- Reinforce with specific feedback

Troubleshooting Signals

- If response is slow: Reduce words, increase wait time
- If partial response: Use proximity for non-responders
- If the signal stops working: Change it (signals lose effectiveness over time)
- If different teachers use different signals: Coordinate or clearly distinguish contexts
- If technology is involved: Always have an unplugged backup

"Smooth transitions are invisible bridges between islands of learning. When students struggle with change, they're not being difficult—they're being human."

Frances Watson-Hester, Ph.D.

Teacher Affirmation

"I am a master of moments between moments. I understand that transitions are where anxiety lives, so I create pathways of predictability and grace, helping my students move through change with confidence and ease."

Transitions That Work

Transition Components

- Clear indication transition is coming (30-second warning)
- Explicit directions for ending the current activity
- Specific instructions for movement or material changes
- Directions for beginning next activity
- Signal for completion

Types of Transitions to Plan

- Entering the room
- Exiting the room
- Switching from one activity to another
- Moving from individual to group work (and back)
- Transitioning to different spaces
- Device transitions (getting out/putting away technology)

Transition Timing

- Use a visible timer for predictability
- Time and chart transitions to create healthy competition with previous records
- Allocate realistic timing in lesson plans
- Build in brief brain breaks during longer transitions
- Practice transitions in isolation when needed

"Organization is not about controlling students—it's about freeing their minds from chaos so they can focus on what truly matters: thinking, creating, and growing."

Frances Watson-Hester, Ph.D.

Teacher Affirmation

"I create order not for the sake of control, but for the gift of clarity. When everything has its place and purpose, my students' mental energy flows toward discovery instead of confusion. I am the curator of an environment where minds can soar."

Managing Materials

Supply Systems

- Community supplies: Reduces forgotten materials, but increases shared responsibility
- Individual supplies: Increases accountability, but requires storage solutions
- Hybrid approach: Community basic supplies, individual specialized items

Storage Solutions

- Clear labeling with words AND visuals
- Consistent location for recurring materials
- Student access levels (open access, limited access, teacher-only access)
- Color-coding by subject or period
- Digital inventory for quickly identifying missing items

Paper Management

- Consistent heading format for all assignments
- Designated location for turning in work
- System for absent student work
- Digital backup requirements for physical assignments
- Regular clean-out sessions (guided for younger students)

"When students work together, magic happens—but only when the teacher has carefully orchestrated the conditions for that magic to flourish."

Frances Watson-Hester, Ph.D.

Teacher Affirmation

"I am a weaver of human connections, bringing together diverse minds and hearts to create something greater than any individual could achieve alone. In my classroom, collaboration isn't just a strategy—it's a celebration of our collective genius."

Group Work Strategies

Forming Effective Groups

- Random grouping: Builds community and flexibility
- Homogeneous grouping: Allows targeted instruction
- Heterogeneous grouping: Provides peer modeling and support
- Interest-based grouping: Increases engagement
- Social-emotional grouping: Addresses relationship dynamics

Role Assignment

- Assign specific roles with clear responsibilities
- Rotate roles regularly to develop diverse skills
- Create visual role cards with specific tasks listed
- Match roles to student strengths initially, then stretch
- Include roles that address management (timekeeper, materials manager)

Accountability Measures

- Individual components within group assignments
- Self and peer evaluation protocols
- Random reporter system (anyone might present)
- Visible progress tracking
- Clear criteria for successful collaboration

"Technology should amplify human connection, not replace it. The digital classroom succeeds when screens become windows to deeper learning, not walls that divide us."

Frances Watson-Hester, Ph.D.

Teacher Affirmation

"I navigate the digital world with intention and wisdom, using technology as a bridge to engagement rather than a barrier to connection. My students learn that screens can enhance our humanity, not diminish it."

Digital Classroom Management

Device Procedures

- Physical placement when not in use (closed, upside down, in designated space)
- Signal for opening/accessing devices
- Screen visibility requirements (angle for teacher viewing)
- Emergency closing procedure (for inappropriate content)
- Battery management expectations

Digital Attention Management

- "Screens up/screens down" signals
- Digital hand-raising systems
- Screen monitoring tools
- Engagement verification techniques
- Distraction minimization settings

Virtual Classroom Strategies

- Clear video/audio expectations
- Participation protocols (chat, hand raising, breakout rooms)
- Visual cues for attention
- Private messaging parameters
- Recording and privacy guidelines

"Your voice carries more than words—it carries your beliefs about your students' potential. Speak to the person they're becoming, not just the behavior you're seeing."

Frances Watson-Hester, Ph.D.

Teacher Affirmation

"My voice is an instrument of transformation. Every word I speak, every tone I choose, plants seeds of possibility in young minds. I speak with the knowledge that my voice may be the one that changes everything for a student today."

Voice and Body Language

Voice Modulation

- Volume levels: Establish a 0-4 scale with specific purposes
- Pacing: Slow down for emphasis, confusion, or emotional moments
- Pitch: Lower for authority, higher for engagement
- Tone: Match to purpose (inviting, firm, curious, enthusiastic)
- Strategic silence: Create space for thinking and self-correction

Body Language Essentials

- Square shoulders toward concerning behavior
- Open posture for discussion and questions
- Move purposefully rather than pacing
- Monitor your facial expressions (especially in frustration)
- Use hand gestures intentionally to emphasize points

Teacher Position Power

- Standing vs. sitting (each sends different messages)
- Eye level conversations for relationship building
- Higher position for direct instruction
- Alongside a position for coaching
- Behind position for building independence

"Sometimes the most powerful intervention requires no words at all—just the quiet presence of someone who cares enough to come close when others might walk away."

Frances Watson-Hester, Ph.D.

Teacher Affirmation

"My presence is my gift. When I move closer to a struggling student, I carry with me years of experience, an ocean of patience, and the unwavering belief that this child matters. Sometimes my proximity speaks louder than my words."

The Power of Proximity

Proximity Planning

- Identify "hot spots" where issues typically arise
- Create pathways that allow natural movement throughout the room
- Position yourself to see all students whenever possible
- Use proximity before behavior escalates
- Combine proximity with affirmation of positive behaviors

Proximity Pitfalls

- Hovering (creates dependency or resentment)
- Proximity only for redirection (creates negative association)
- Predictable patterns (students time their behavior)
- Cultural sensitivity concerns (respect personal space differences)
- Ignoring distant corners of the room

Proximity Advantages

- Non-verbal intervention without disrupting flow
- Opportunity to provide individual feedback
- Demonstrates awareness of the entire classroom
- Builds relationships through brief connections
- Provides data on student progress and needs

"Minor disruptions are often major opportunities disguised. The student who interrupts may be the one who needs connection most desperately."

Frances Watson-Hester, Ph.D.

Teacher Affirmation

"I see beneath the surface of challenging behaviors to the human need underneath. What others might label as disruption, I recognize as communication. Every difficult moment is an invitation to build a bridge toward understanding."

Addressing Minor Disruptions

Least Invasive Interventions

- Nonverbal cue
- Proximity
- Anonymous group reminder
- Private individual reminder
- Lightning-quick redirect
- Brief private conversation

The Art of Redirection

- Address behavior, not character
- Provide specific positive replacement behavior
- Assume positive intent initially
- Redirect privately whenever possible
- Keep interactions brief and non-emotional

Prevention Through Engagement

- Identify early warning signs of disengagement
- Increase participation rate through structured protocols
- Use engagement data to adjust pacing
- Incorporate movement strategically
- Plan "high engagement" activities for vulnerable periods (after lunch, end of day)

"In moments of escalation, your calm becomes their compass. When storms rage in young hearts, be the lighthouse—steady, visible, and unwavering."

Frances Watson-Hester, Ph.D.

Teacher Affirmation

"I am the calm in my students' storms. When emotions run high and logic runs low, my steady presence becomes their anchor. I breathe peace into chaos and offer hope when despair threatens to overwhelm."

De-escalation Techniques

Early Warning Signs

- Change in voice volume/tone
- Physical restlessness
- Verbal refusal or defiance
- Withdrawal from participation
- Unusual interaction patterns with peers

De-escalation Protocol

- Remain calm and emotionally neutral
- Create space (physical and emotional)
- Use simple, clear language
- Offer limited choices within boundaries
- Focus on next steps rather than past actions

Recovery Process

- Provide cool-down time and space
- Use reflection tools appropriate to the age
- Facilitate restoration of relationships
- Identify triggers and warning signs for the future
- Create a success plan for similar situations

"Accountability without support is punishment. Support without accountability is enabling. True education requires both—wrapped in unconditional belief in student potential."

Frances Watson-Hester, Ph.D.

Teacher Affirmation

"I hold high expectations and high support in perfect balance. I believe in my students' capacity to grow, to learn, and to rise to meet challenges. My accountability comes from love, not judgment—from hope, not condemnation."

Promoting Student Accountability

Self-Monitoring Tools

- Goal-setting templates with student-friendly language
- Visual progress trackers
- Reflection protocols
- Self-evaluation rubrics
- Digital productivity tools

Peer Accountability Systems

- Structured protocols for peer feedback
- Partner check systems
- Group contribution evaluations
- Peer teaching opportunities
- Collaborative problem-solving frameworks

Increasing Independence Progressively

- Scaffold responsibility with gradual release
- Create visual guides for independent problem-solving
- Establish "ask three before me" protocol
- Implement student-led routines
- Celebrate independence milestones

"Relationships are not the soft skill of education—they are the foundation upon which all learning stands. Academic rigor without relational trust is like building skyscrapers on sand."

Frances Watson-Hester, Ph.D.

Teacher Affirmation

"I am a relationship architect, building bridges of trust that can bear the weight of academic challenge and personal growth. My students learn best because they feel known, valued, and believed in. Connection precedes correction, always."

Building Student Relationships

Relationship-Building Priorities

- Learn personal interests beyond academics
- Notice and acknowledge changes (haircut, new glasses, mood shifts)
- Connect curriculum to student interests
- Attend extracurricular events when possible
- Share appropriate personal connections to content

Repair After Difficult Interactions

- Address the incident privately
- Separate the behavior from the student's worth
- Take responsibility for your contribution
- Collaboratively develop solutions
- End with a positive connection

Small Moments That Matter

- Greeting by name daily
- Brief check-ins during independent work
- Specific encouragement (beyond "good job")
- Remembering personal details
- Following up on previous conversations
- Ask students about things that matter to them.

"There are no difficult students—only students whose needs we haven't yet learned to meet. Every personality in your classroom is a puzzle worth solving."

Frances Watson-Hester, Ph.D.

Teacher Affirmation

"I am a student of my students, constantly learning how to reach each unique mind and heart in my care. Where others see difficulty, I see complexity. Where others see problems, I see potential waiting to be unlocked."

Managing Different Personalities

The Quiet Student

- Provide alternative participation formats
- Use think-pair-share to build confidence
- Check understanding privately
- Create small group leadership opportunities
- Honor their processing style

The Energetic Student

- Provide legitimate movement opportunities
- Assign classroom jobs requiring energy
- Use proximity to provide calm
- Teach self-monitoring techniques
- Channel enthusiasm productively

The Challenging Student

- Identify potential triggers proactively
- Establish private communication signals
- Create success-oriented roles
- Schedule regular positive check-ins
- Collaborate on personalized strategies

The Perfectionistic Student

- Focus on growth over performance
- Set reasonable time limits

- Teach healthy revision processes
- Normalize mistakes as learning
- Model managing imperfection

"Communication is not about perfect words—it's about perfect intention. When students feel heard and valued, even imperfect messages can inspire transformational learning."

Frances Watson-Hester, Ph.D.

Teacher Affirmation

"I communicate with my whole heart, knowing that my intention matters more than my eloquence. My students hear not just my words, but my care, my respect, and my unwavering belief in their ability to understand and grow."

Clear Communication

Giving Directions
- Gain full attention before beginning
- Break complex directions into steps
- Provide visual supports
- Check for understanding
- Have students rephrase instructions

Asking Effective Questions
- Plan questions at different cognitive levels
- Use appropriate wait time (3-5 seconds minimum)
- Implement "no hands" protocols periodically
- Create participation tracking systems
- Balance recall and higher-order thinking

Providing Feedback
- Be specific and actionable
- Connect to clear criteria
- Balance reinforcement and correction
- Consider timing for maximum impact
- Differentiate delivery method based on student needs

"Time is the most democratic resource we have—every student gets the same 24 hours. How we steward those precious classroom minutes determines whether dreams take flight or remain grounded."

Frances Watson-Hester, Ph.D.

Teacher Affirmation

"I am a guardian of precious time, knowing that every minute in my classroom is a gift that cannot be returned or replaced. I use our time together intentionally, purposefully, and with reverence for the opportunity to shape young minds."

Time Management Mastery

Lesson Pacing

- Plan timing by segment with buffers
- Use visible timers for transparency
- Develop signals for extending or contracting activities
- Create "must do" and "may do" components
- Build in processing time for complex concepts

Maximizing Instructional Minutes

- Develop "sponge" activities for transitions and unexpected time
- Create entry routines that begin learning immediately
- Implement exit routines that continue until dismissal
- Use tiered assignments for early finishers
- Track and eliminate recurring time-wasters

Managing Administrative Tasks

- Batch similar tasks (grading, emails, planning)
- Create templates for recurring communication
- Develop student jobs for appropriate tasks
- Implement digital efficiency tools
- Schedule focused work during high-energy times

"Parents are not the audience for your educational performance—they are partners in the most important work of shaping young minds. When we work together, children soar."

Frances Watson-Hester, Ph.D.

Teacher Affirmation

"I welcome parents as co-authors in their child's educational story. Together, we form a circle of support that surrounds each student with consistent love, high expectations, and unwavering belief in their potential to succeed."

Parent Partnerships

Communication Systems

- Establish preferred contact methods (email, phone, platform)
- Set clear boundaries for response times
- Create templates for recurring updates
- Differentiate urgent vs. non-urgent channels
- Provide language support when needed

Difficult Conversations

- Begin with shared goals
- Use objective, documentable observations
- Focus on next steps rather than past issues
- Summarize action items and responsibilities
- Schedule follow-up check-ins

Building Positive Connections

- Initiate positive contact before problems arise
- Learn about family priorities and values
- Create participation opportunities that respect diverse schedules
- Share student successes specifically
- Express genuine appreciation for support

"Cultural responsiveness is not about changing who you are—it's about expanding who you can become. Every student's background is a gift that enriches our shared learning journey."

Frances Watson-Hester, Ph.D.

Teacher Affirmation

"I celebrate the beautiful diversity that walks through my door each day. My students' cultures, languages, and experiences don't complicate my teaching—they complete it. I am constantly learning, growing, and becoming more than I was yesterday."

Cultural Responsiveness

Building Cultural Knowledge

- Learn about communities represented in your classroom
- Identify cultural differences in communication styles
- Recognize varied expectations around authority
- Understand family structures and values
- Acknowledge cultural strengths

Adapting Management Approaches

- Consider cultural interpretations of eye contact, voice volume, and physical space
- Recognize that silence may indicate respect, not disengagement
- Provide multiple pathways for participation
- Use culturally familiar examples and references
- Include diverse perspectives in classroom content

Examining Personal Bias

- Notice patterns in your response to behaviors
- Question assumptions about "appropriate" behavior
- Identify areas where your cultural background influences expectations
- Seek feedback from cultural bridges
- Commit to ongoing learning and adaptation

"Trauma-informed teaching is not about lowering expectations—it's about understanding that the path to high achievement may look different for each child. Healing and learning walk hand in hand."

Frances Watson-Hester, Ph.D.

Teacher Affirmation

"I see past the armor that pain sometimes creates to the tender heart beneath. My classroom is a sanctuary where wounds can heal and spirits can soar. I hold space for both struggle and triumph, knowing that each child's journey is sacred."

Trauma-Informed Approaches

Understanding Trauma Responses

- Fight: Argumentative, defiant, aggressive behaviors
- Flight: Withdrawal, avoidance, escaping situations
- Freeze: Shutting down, appearing "zoned out"
- Fawn: People-pleasing, excessive compliance
- Combinations: Many students show mixed responses

Creating Trauma-Sensitive Environments

- Establish predictable routines and transitions
- Provide regulatory supports (fidgets, calming corner, breaks)
- Teach emotional vocabulary explicitly
- Create safety through choice and control when possible
- Balance flexibility with consistency

De-escalation Specifics for Trauma

- Maintain calm presence through co-regulation
- Avoid power struggles and ultimatums
- Create space without isolation
- Use simple, concrete language
- Focus on safety in the moment before processing

"You cannot pour from an empty cup, and education demands everything you have to give. Self-care is not selfish—it's strategic. Your well-being is a professional responsibility."

Frances Watson-Hester, Ph.D.

Teacher Affirmation

"I honor my own humanity while serving others. My well-being matters not just for me, but for every student whose life I touch. When I care for myself, I model for my students what it means to value the vessel that carries such important work."

Self-Care and Sustainability

Daily Practices

- Create beginning and ending rituals for the workday
- Schedule short breaks for basic needs
- Practice strategic detachment from student behaviors
- Identify energy-giving versus energy-draining activities
- Implement one mindfulness practice daily

Weekly Resets

- Limit weekend work to a specific timeframe
- Schedule complete disconnection from school
- Engage in physical activity
- Connect with supportive colleagues
- Reflect on successes, not just challenges

Managing Emotional Labor

- Recognize signs of compassion fatigue
- Develop transition practices between home and school
- Create boundaries around school communication
- Find healthy emotional processing outlets
- Seek professional support when needed

"In crisis, we discover what we truly value. Prepare not just procedures, but principles—when emergency strikes, let your deepest convictions about student worth guide every decision."

Frances Watson-Hester, Ph.D.

Teacher Affirmation

"I am prepared not just with protocols, but with purpose. In moments of crisis, my love for my students guides my actions. I am their protector, their calm in chaos, their reminder that even in uncertainty, they are safe and valued."

Frances Watson Hester, Ph.D.

Emergency Responses

Physical Safety Emergencies

- Know the official protocols for your building
- Establish clear student expectations for each scenario
- Create accessible emergency lesson plans
- Assign student roles when appropriate
- Practice responses regularly

Emotional/Behavioral Crises

- Identify resources available (counselor, administrator, social worker)
- Develop clear signals for urgent assistance
- Create a classroom evacuation plan if needed
- Know reporting requirements for serious concerns
- Prepare follow-up plans for the class after incidents

Substitute Teacher Preparation

- Create clear procedures documentation
- Prepare emergency sub plans
- Train reliable student leaders
- Establish a communication channel for urgent concerns
- Set expectations for student behavior with substitutes

"Teaching is the profession that creates all other professions. In your hands lies the power to shape not just minds, but the future itself. Never underestimate the sacred trust you carry."*

Frances Watson-Hester, Ph.D.

Teacher Affirmation

"I am entrusted with the most important work in the world: nurturing the minds and hearts that will shape tomorrow. Every lesson I teach, every relationship I build, every moment of care I offer ripples forward into a future I may never see, but will help create."

Final Thoughts

Classroom management is both science and art. The strategies in this book provide a foundation, but your relationships with students will ultimately determine your success. Remember these final truths:

Your credibility comes from consistency, not perfection Management flows from a genuine connection with students Systems serve learning, not control Flexibility within structure creates resilience Your well-being directly impacts classroom climate

Keep this book close, but hold your principles closer. Trust your instincts, seek continuous growth, and remember why you chose this profession. Your influence extends far beyond what you can see in any given moment.

The strategies in this book were developed through decades of classroom experience, research, and collaboration with master teachers. They represent practical wisdom that transcends educational trends while acknowledging the evolving nature of teaching and learning.

"Always begin with the end in mind." Steven Covey

NOTES

NOTES

NOTES

Frances Watson Hester, Ph.D.

NOTES

NOTES

NOTES

NOTES

Frances Watson Hester, Ph.D.

NOTES

NOTES

Frances Watson Hester, Ph.D.

NOTES

www.ingramcontent.com/pod-product-compliance
Lightning Source LLC
Chambersburg PA
CBHW050330010526
44119CB00050B/739